DIRECTIONS IN DEVELOPMENT

GW00725757

Water Supply, Sanitation, and Environmental Sustainability
The Financing Challenge

Ismail Serageldin

The World Bank
Washington, D.C.

© 1994 The International Bank for Reconstruction
and Development/THE WORLD BANK
1818 H Street, N.W.
Washington, D.C. 20433

The findings, interpretations, and conclusions expressed in this study are
entirely those of the author and should not be attributed in any manner to
the World Bank, to its affiliated organizations, or to members of its Board of
Executive Directors or the countries they represent.

Cover photograph of an inlet of the Mediterranean Sea along the coast of
Tunisia, by Curt Carnemark.

Library of Congress Cataloging-in-Publication Data

Serageldin, Ismail, 1944–
    Water supply, sanitation, and environmental sustainability: the
financing challenge / Ismail Serageldin.
        p.   cm. — (Directions in development)
    Includes bibliographical references (p.   ).
    ISBN 0-8213-3022-5
    1. Sewage disposal—Developing countries—Finance.   2. Water
supply—Developing countries—Finance.   3. Sewage—Environmental
aspects—Developing countries.   4. Sanitation—Developing countries.
5. Public health—Developing countries.   I. Title.   II. Series:
Directions in development (Washington, D.C.)
HD4480.D44S47   1994
338.4'3363728'091724—dc20   94-34389
                                                                                          CIP

Contents

Foreword

This booklet is an adaptation of my keynote address to the Ministerial Conference, "Drinking Water and Environmental Sanitation: Implementing *Agenda 21*," held in Noordwijk, The Netherlands, on March 22, 1994, under the sponsorship of the government of the Netherlands. This topic comprises probably the most immediate set of environmental issues facing billions of people in developing countries.

This statement does not do justice to the environmental and political aspects of water supply and sanitation because I was asked to concentrate specifically on the financing aspects—issues with which the World Bank has long and varied experience and that must be confronted if we are to have any hope of solving the other challenges in the water supply sector.

The presentation in this booklet distinguishes between an "old agenda" of providing household water and sanitation services to large numbers of people and a "new agenda" that requires sustainable, environmentally sensitive use of water resources. The challenge facing developing countries—and the multilateral agencies that support their development efforts—is to attend to the new agenda even while continuing to address forcefully the uncompleted old one. This will require adopting a "new view"—endorsed at the International Conference on Water and the Environment held in Dublin in 1992—that sees water as an economic good and calls for a participatory approach to management of this (by definition, scarce) resource, a view that goes beyond the old view that left provision of services largely up to governments. This new view entrusts consumers and neighborhoods with a large say regarding the services they want and how to pay for them. It therefore gives the actual users much more choice, as well as responsibility, than did the old top-down approach. It means that the poor— who are often left out of theoretically universal arrangements that mainly benefit and subsidize nonpoor users—can gain access to the services they want and receive targeted support from governments. And as a growing body of experience reveals, this new view offers the best hope for dealing with both the old and the new agendas.

In various countries and in different social and physical contexts, the new approach based on economic incentives and participatory decisionmaking is being used—whether by a neighborhood, a city, or a region—to bring services to the people who need them. This booklet describes some of these promising initiatives and examines the general principles that underlie them. It looks at how the World Bank and other agencies can assist and encourage efforts to meet the challenge of providing environmentally sustainable water and sanitation services to growing populations that expect and have a right to decent living conditions.

Ismail Serageldin
Vice President
for Environmentally Sustainable Development
The World Bank

Acknowledgments

The author is grateful to John Briscoe, Chief of the World Bank's Water and Sanitation Division, and Guy Le Moigne, Senior Water Resources Advisor, for their help in preparing this paper. Editorial and production assistance was provided by Laurie Edwards, David Kinley, Nancy Levine, Stephanie Gerard, Cindy Stock, and Michael Wishart.

Summary

The water supply and sanitation sector faces two great challenges in developing countries.

The first challenge is to complete the "old agenda" of providing household services. Although considerable progress has been made, much remains to be done. A billion people still lack access to an adequate supply of water, and 1.7 billion do not have adequate sanitation facilities. Furthermore, the quality and reliability of existing services are often unacceptable. To compound the situation, the costs of providing services are rising substantially because of rapid urbanization, mismanagement of water resources, and the low efficiency of many water supply organizations.

Over the past thirty years developing countries have allocated an increasing share of their gross domestic product (GDP) to public spending on the provision of water and sanitation services. It would appear that the proportion of public spending on these household services has been too high, for three reasons. First, the low contribution of users has meant that supply agencies are not accountable to consumers. Second, these resources have been used primarily to subsidize services to the middle class and the rich. Third, spending on household services has left few public resources available for wastewater treatment and management.

The second challenge is the "new agenda" of environmentally sustainable development. In some respects—high costs and limited resources—the situation confronting developing countries is similar to that faced by industrial countries. But in other respects the task for developing countries is considerably more difficult: water in developing countries is much more seriously degraded and is deteriorating rapidly; far fewer financial resources are available for environmental protection; and institutional capacity is weaker.

Completing the old agenda and addressing the new agenda constitute a daunting challenge for developing countries. This book describes some of the more imaginative and promising approaches to addressing these challenges at different levels, ranging from self-financed sewers in a squatter settlement in Karachi, Pakistan, to the emergence of participatory river basin management in Brazil. From such promising experiences, two central elements can be discerned.

- *Institutions.* The promising institutional arrangements are ones in which the people who are affected are put in charge of decisions regarding both environmental services and the resources to be spent on them. At the lowest level this means letting households choose the services they want and are willing to pay for. At the highest level it means that the stakeholders in a river basin decide what level of environmental quality they want and are willing to pay for. Consistent with this participatory thrust is the dictum that decisionmaking responsibility should be moved to the lowest appropriate level. Thus, for instance, river basin authorities should concentrate on managing abstraction (the removal of water from a shared source) and pollution externalities and let municipalities decide how to manage their water and sewerage services most effectively. This inevitably means a more sharply defined role for government and broader participation of the private sector and nongovernmental organizations.
- *Instruments.* The other central element is to make more extensive use of market-like instruments at all levels. At the household level this means much greater reliance on user charges for raising revenues and enhancing accountability and efficiency. At the service level it means greater reliance on the private sector for provision. And at the river basin level it means greater use of abstraction charges, pollution charges, and water markets for water resource management.

Formidable as the challenges are, there is hope that progress can be made, not least because of the remarkable consensus that is emerging among many of the partners involved—official and nonofficial—concerning this new paradigm for environmentally sustainable and equitable development of the water and sanitation sector. The task now is to turn this vision into the reality of better services and a better environment for people.

The Financing Challenge

Water sector development is immediately relevant for billions of people in developing countries and for the quality of the environment in which they live. Financing such development in a responsive, responsible, and sustainable way is a challenge we must meet successfully. The challenge is twofold. First, there is the "old agenda" of providing all people of the world with adequate water supply and sanitation services. Second, there is the challenge of the "new agenda," which requires that much greater attention be paid to ensuring that our use of water resources is sustainable in terms of both quality and quantity.

The "Old Agenda": Provision of Household Water and Sanitation Services

Figure 1 compares water supply and sanitation coverage in developing countries in 1980 and 1990. In interpreting these data it is instructive to view the glass in two ways: as half full and as half empty.

If we look at the glass as half full, we can take considerable satisfaction from the progress we have made in meeting the challenge. Over the course of the 1980s, an additional 1.6 billion people were provided access to water of reasonable quality; the number of urban people with access to an adequate water supply increased by about 80 percent; and the number of urban people with adequate sanitation facilities increased by about 50 percent.

If we look at the glass as half empty, we can see that an enormous challenge remains: 1 billion people still lack access to an adequate supply of water, and 1.7 billion do not have adequate sanitation facilities. And in urban areas the number of people without access to adequate sanitation actually increased by about 70 million during the 1980s.

The most obvious and poignant costs of these service shortfalls are those measured in human suffering. What we see with our eyes is confirmed by the numbers we collect. We have abundant evidence of the huge costs of not providing access. In city after city in the developing world, those who are not served, especially the poor in urban areas, often pay high costs. These poor often rely on vendors who typically charge $2 to $3 for a cubic meter of water—ten or more times the price paid by the served for water from a tap in their houses. And, as shown

Figure 1. Access to Safe Water and Adequate Sanitation in Developing Countries, 1980 and 1990

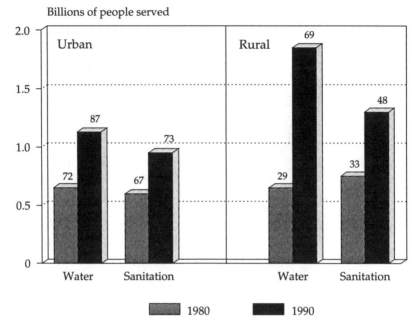

Note: Numbers above the bars are percentages of the relevant population
Source: Adapted from World Bank 1992d.

in table 1, the health consequences are staggering—an estimated 2 million deaths from diarrhea alone could be avoided each year if all people had access to satisfactory water supply and sanitation services.

The Emerging "New Agenda"

While the old agenda with its focus on household services still poses large financial, technical, and institutional challenges, a new agenda that emphasizes environmentally sustainable development has emerged forcefully—and appropriately—in recent years. This concern extends to both the quantity and the quality of surface water and groundwater.

The quality of the aquatic environment is a global concern, but the situation in cities in developing countries is especially acute. Even in middle-income countries sewage is rarely treated. Buenos Aires, for instance, treats only 2 percent of its sewage—a figure that is typical for the middle-income countries of Latin America. As shown in figure 2, water quality is far worse in developing than in industrial countries.

Table 1. Effects of Improved Water and Sanitation on Sickness

Disease	Millions affected by illness	Median reduction attributable to improvement (percent)
Diarrhea	900[a]	22
Roundworm	900	28
Guinea worm	4	76
Schistosomiasis	200	73

a. Refers to number of episodes in a year.
Source: World Bank 1992d.

Furthermore, while environmental quality in industrial countries improved over the 1980s, it did not improve in middle-income countries, and it declined sharply in low-income countries.

The costs of this degradation can be seen in many ways. Most rivers in and around cities and towns in developing countries are little more than open, stinking sewers that not only degrade the aesthetic life of the city but also constitute a reservoir for cholera and other water-related diseases. And as the "urban shadow" of pollution spreads con-

Figure 2. Dissolved Oxygen Levels in Rivers in Developing and Industrial Countries

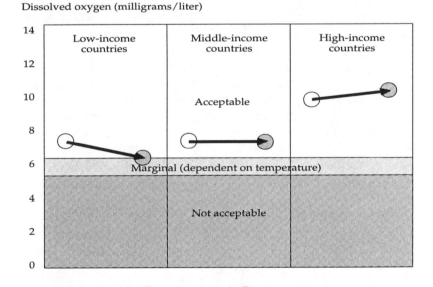

Dissolved oxygen (milligrams/liter)

Source: World Bank 1992d.

centrically around a city, expensive adaptations are required so that water supplies can remain safe. To take just one case, Shanghai had to move its water supply intake 40 kilometers upstream at a cost of $300 million because of the degradation of river water quality around the city.

In this nexus of service and environmental issues, it is instructive to consider the sequence in which people demand water supply and sanitation services. Consider, for instance, a family that migrates to a shantytown. Their first environmental priority is to secure an adequate water supply at reasonable cost. This is followed shortly by the need to secure a private, convenient, and sanitary place for defecation. Families show a high willingness to pay for these household or private services, in part because the alternatives are so unsatisfactory and so costly. They put substantial pressure on local and national governments to provide such services, and it is natural and appropriate that the bulk of external assistance in the early stages of development goes to meeting this strong demand. The very success in meeting these primary needs, however, gives rise to a second generation of demands— for removal of wastewater from the household, then from the neighborhood, and finally from the city. And success in this important endeavor gives rise to another problem: the protection of the environment from the degrading effects of large amounts of waterborne waste.

A number of implications emanate from this description. To begin with, the historic "bias" in favor of water (at the expense of sanitation and sewerage) is probably not only not "wrong," as is currently often implied, but actually right! The historical experience of industrial countries and the contemporary experience of developing countries demonstrate clearly that only when the first challenge (the provision of services) has been substantially met do households and societies pay attention to the "higher-order" challenges of environmental protection. Thus it is not surprising, and not incorrect, that the portfolios of external assistance agencies have concentrated on the provision of water supply (see World Bank 1993b, pp. 95ff). For example, of World Bank lending for water and sanitation over the past thirty years, only about 15 percent has been for sanitation and sewerage, with most of this amount spent on sewage collection and only a small fraction spent on treatment. Boxes 1 and 2 demonstrate graphically how forcefully poor people demand environmental services once the primary need for water supply has been met.

Financing

Developing countries face the formidable double-barreled challenge of completing the old agenda and making progress on the new agenda. In

Box 1. Meeting the Demand for Sanitation Services: The Orangi Pilot Project, Karachi

When in the early 1980s Akhter Hameed Khan, a world-renowned community organizer, began working in the slums of Karachi, he found that people in this area had a relatively satisfactory supply of water but that the streets were "filled with excreta and waste water, making movement difficult and creating enormous health hazards." What did the people who lived there want, and how did they intend to get it? Dr. Khan asked. What they wanted was clear: "people aspired to a traditional sewerage system . . . it would be difficult to get them to finance anything else." And how they would get it, too, was clear—they would have Dr. Khan persuade the Karachi Development Authority (KDA) to provide it for free, as it did (or so they perceived) for the richer areas of the city.

Dr. Khan spent months going with representatives from the community to petition the KDA to provide the service. Once it was apparent that this would never happen, Dr. Khan was ready to work with the community in finding alternatives. (He would later describe this first step as the most important thing he did in Orangi—liberating, as he put it, the people from the demobilizing myths of government promises.)

With a small amount of core external funding, the Orangi Pilot Project (OPP) was started. It was clear which services people wanted; the task was to reduce the costs so the services would be affordable and to develop organizations that could provide and operate the systems. On the technical side the achievements of the OPP architects and engineers were remarkable and innovative. In part thanks to the elimination of corruption and the provision of labor by community members, the costs (in-house sanitary latrine and house sewer on the plot and underground sewers in the lanes and streets) are less than $100 per household.

The local organizational achievements are equally impressive. OPP staff members have played a catalytic role: they explain the benefits of sanitation and the technical possibilities to residents, conduct research, and provide technical assistance. Staff members never handle the community's money. (Even in the project's early years the total costs of OPP's operations amounted to less than 15 percent of the amount invested by the community.)

Households' responsibilities include financing their share of the costs, participating in construction, and electing a "lane manager" who typically represents about fifteen households. The lane committees, in turn, elect members of neighborhood committees (usually representing around 600 houses) who manage the secondary sewers. The early successes achieved by the project created a "snowball" effect, in part because of increases in the value of property where lanes had installed a sewerage system. As the power of the OPP-related organizations increased, they were able to bring pressure on the municipality to provide funds for the construction of secondary and primary sewers.

(Box continues on the following page.)

Box 1 (*continued*)

The Orangi Pilot Project has led to the provision of sewerage to more than 600,000 poor people in Karachi. At least one progressive municipal development authority in Pakistan is seeking to follow the OPP method and, in the words of Arif Hasan of the Orangi Pilot Project, "to have government behave like [a nongovernmental organization]." Even in Karachi the mayor has now formally accepted the principle of "internal" development by the residents and "external" development (including the trunk sewers and treatment) by the municipality.

The experience of Orangi demonstrates graphically how people's demands move naturally from the provision of water to removal of waste from their houses, then from their blocks, and, finally, from their neighborhood and town.

Source: Hasan 1986.

---

this section we examine these challenges from a financing perspective by asking three questions:

- What do services cost, and how is this changing?
- Should public spending be increased?
- What are the central elements in a financially sustainable approach to these challenges?

What Do Services Cost, and How Are the Costs Changing?

THE OLD AGENDA.   Real costs of water supply and sanitation services are changing for several reasons. First are demographic and economic factors. As the population of developing countries becomes more urbanized, per capita costs rise. This is partly because a number of low-cost, on-site urban sanitation technologies (see table 2) become infeasible in dense urban settlements and partly because urban people—as demonstrated in the Orangi and São Paulo cases—aspire to having a high level of service.

Second are resource factors. Today twenty-two countries have renewable water resources of less than 1,000 cubic meters per capita—a level commonly taken to indicate severe water scarcity—and an additional eighteen countries have less than 2,000 cubic meters per capita. Elsewhere, water scarcity is less of a problem at the national level but is nevertheless severe in certain regions, at certain times of the year, and during periods of drought. The effects of these "natural" factors are seriously exacerbated by the widespread mismanagement of water re-

---

Box 2. Meeting the Demand for Sanitation Services: The *Favelas* of São Paulo

In the 1980s the Brazilian city of São Paulo made extraordinary progress in providing all its residents with water supply and sanitation services. In 1980 just 32 percent of the *favelas* (low-income, informal settlements) had a piped water supply, and less than 1 percent had a sewerage system. By 1990 the respective figures were 99 percent and 15 percent!

SABESP, the state water utility serving São Paulo, is a technically sophisticated water supply organization. Until the emergence of democracy in Brazil, SABESP had defined its role narrowly and technocratically. Specifically, it did not consider provision of services to the *favelas* to be its responsibility because it was not able to do this according to its prescribed technical standards and because the *favelas* were not "legal," and it resisted pressures to provide services to the settlements. Meanwhile, a small municipal agency (COBES) was experimenting with new technical and institutional ways of providing water and sanitation services to the poor. On the technical side this did not involve provision of inferior service but reduction of the cost of providing in-house services by using plastic pipe and servicing narrow roads where access was limited. On the institutional side the community had to assume significant responsibility for community relations and for supervising the work of the contractors.

As the military regime withdrew and was replaced by democratic politics in the early 1980s, the pressures on SABESP to serve the *favelas* increased. Community pressure was channeled through the municipal agencies and responsive officials and politicians, including the mayor and governor. Since COBES had shown how it was, in fact, possible to serve the favelas, SABESP had no option but to respond.

The lessons from São Paulo are twofold. First, that once the poor have water services, a strong demand for sanitation services naturally emerges. Second, where institutions are responsive and innovative, major gains can be made in the provision of these services at full cost to poor people.

---

sources, with scarcity induced by the provision of large quantities of water at minimal or no cost for low-value agricultural uses. Another influence on costs is that cities have first sought water where it is easiest and cheapest to obtain, and as they grow, the "pollution shadows" around them often engulf existing water intakes, necessitating expensive relocation of intakes (as illustrated by the Shanghai case described earlier). The compound effect of these factors is, as illustrated in figure 3, a large increase in the costs of capturing water of adequate quality and transporting it to cities and towns.

Table 2. Typical Investment Costs for Different Levels of Service

(approximate U.S. dollar value)

	Rural	Urban	
	Low	Intermediate	High
Water supply	10[a]	100[b]	200[c]
Sanitation	104[d]	255[d]	3,506[e]

a. Handpump or standpump.
b. Public standpipe.
c. Piped water, house connection.
d. Pour-flush or ventilated, improved pit latrines.
e. Piped sewerage with treatment.
Source: World Bank 1992d.

Figure 3. How the Cost of Supplying Water Is Increasing

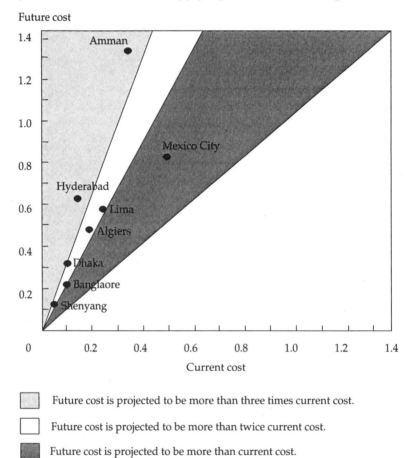

Future cost

Current cost

Future cost is projected to be more than three times current cost.

Future cost is projected to be more than twice current cost.

Future cost is projected to be more than current cost.

Source: World Bank 1992d.

Widespread inefficiency in supplying water and sanitation is a major factor in the high cost of water sector services, as is documented in a recent World Bank study. The study, which examined more than 120 urban water projects initiated between 1967 and 1989, concludes that despite efforts at capacity building for the public institutions concerned, only in four countries—Botswana, the Republic of Korea, Singapore, and Tunisia—have public water and sewerage utilities reached acceptable levels of performance.

A few examples illustrate how serious the situation is:

- In Caracas and Mexico City an estimated 30 percent of connections are not registered.
- Unaccounted-for water is 8 percent of total water supply in Singapore but 58 percent in Manila and about 40 percent in most Latin American cities. For Latin America as a whole, such water losses cost between $1 billion and $1.5 billion in revenue forgone every year.
- The number of employees per 1,000 water connections is between two and three in Western Europe and about four in a well-run developing country utility (Santiago, Chile), but between ten and twenty in most Latin American utilities.

Figure 4. Degree of Cost Recovery in Infrastructure Sectors in Developing Countries

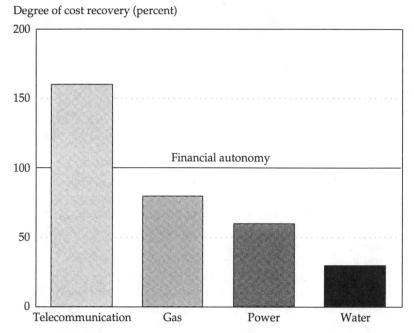

Degree of cost recovery (percent)

Source: World Bank 1994.

The financial performance of water and sewerage agencies is equally poor and, as shown in figure 4, much worse than for other infrastructure sectors. A recent World Bank review showed that public utilities in developing countries seldom recovered all of their costs from users. The shortfalls have to be met by large injections of public money. In Brazil between the mid-1970s and the mid-1980s, about $1 billion of public cash was invested in the water sector annually. The federal subsidy for water and sewerage services to Mexico City amounts to more than $1 billion a year, or 0.6 percent of gross domestic product (GDP). The overall picture is clear—most public water utilities in developing countries are high-cost, low-quality producers of services.

The performance of most rural water supply agencies has also been generally poor. A common approach has been for governments to limit services by supporting only low-cost technologies (such as improved pit latrines and handpumps). While the development of low-cost, robust technologies of this sort is vital, a key mistake made in many programs has been to restrict the choices available to people. This paternalistic approach has proved highly counterproductive. The fundamental reason is that the services offered have not corresponded to those which people—including poor people—want and are willing to pay for. In many instances this has led to a "low-level equilibrium trap" in which people are not willing to pay for what they see as an unsatisfactory service. The result is that resources for the operation and maintenance of the service are not generated, and the quality of service declines still further.

The lessons are clear. From a demand perspective, the message is that people must be trusted to choose, from a menu of service levels, those services they want and are willing to pay for. From a supply perspective, the lesson is that rigorous attention must be paid to providing households with a particular level of service at the lowest possible cost.

THE NEW AGENDA.   Collecting and treating sewage is a very expensive business. Typical investment costs for collecting sewage from a household are on the order of $1,000. Treatment costs (see figure 5) typically increase the cost to about $1,500, just for primary treatment. For higher levels of treatment (as now mandated in industrial countries), costs are much higher.

In the aggregate, the costs of meeting the new agenda can be huge. To cite just one example, it is estimated that the United Kingdom will have to invest about $60 billion in wastewater treatment over the next decade in order to meet the new European water quality standards. This amounts to about $1,000 per capita, or about 0.6 percent of GDP spent on wastewater treatment alone over that ten-year period.

Compounding this already formidable picture is the fact that sewerage services in developing countries have been managed with even less efficiency than water services. In Accra, for instance, only 130 con-

Figure 5. The Costs of Different Types of Sewage Treatment

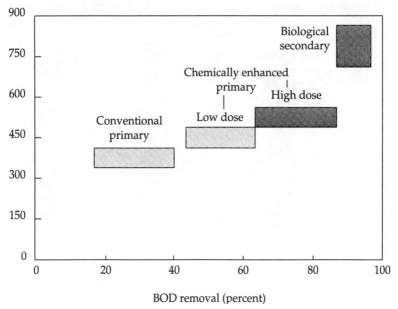

Total cost (dollars per household)

BOD removal (percent)

Note: The assumptions made are that per capita consumption is 160 liters per day and household size is five persons.
Source: U.S. Natural Research Council 1994.

nections were made to a sewerage system designed to serve 2,000 connections. And in Mexico it is estimated that less than 10 percent of sewage treatment plants are operated satisfactorily.

Should Public Spending in the Water Sector Be Increased?

Two recent assessments by the World Bank provide a clear overview of public financing for the water and sanitation sector in developing countries over the past three decades. As shown in figure 6, the proportion of GDP invested in water supply and sanitation rose from about 0.25 percent in the 1960s to about 0.45 percent in the 1980s. Furthermore, although it was widely believed that the allocation to the sector fell during the difficult years of the late 1980s, a World Bank analysis of information from public investment reviews in twenty-nine countries showed a different picture. Overall public investment did indeed decline, from 10.9 percent of GDP in 1985 to 8.7 percent in 1988, but over this same period, investment in water and sanitation held virtually constant at about 0.4 percent of GDP.

Figure 6. Public Investment in Infrastructure in Developing Countries over Three Decades

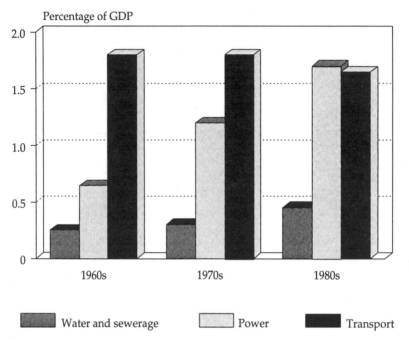

Percentage of GDP

| | Water and sewerage | | Power | | Transport |

Source: World Bank data.

THE LARGE "HIDDEN" WATER ECONOMY. Especially where formal institutions perform least adequately, a large informal, private industry has arisen to meet those needs that are not adequately served by formal institutions.

In Jakarta only 14 percent of the 8 million people living in the city receive piped water directly. About 32 percent purchase water from street vendors, and the remaining 54 percent rely on private wells. There are in the city more than 800,000 septic tanks, installed by local contractors, fully financed by households themselves, and maintained by a thriving and competitive service industry.

In cities throughout the developing world households cope with the unreliability of formal water supply service by building in-house storage tanks, installing booster pumps (which can draw contaminated groundwater into the water distribution system), and sinking wells. In Tegucigalpa, Honduras, the amount spent on such investments would be enough to double the number of deep wells currently providing water to the city. The size of this informal and often hidden water economy often dwarfs the size of the visible water economy. In Onitsha, Nigeria, for instance, revenues collected by water vendors are about ten times the revenues collected by the formal water utility!

In rural areas, too, the hidden water economy is often huge. In Pakistan more than 3 million families have wells fitted with pumps, many of which are motorized. The wells are paid for in full by the families, and all equipment is provided and serviced by a vibrant local private sector industry.

The degree of distortion involved in ignoring the informal provision and financing of water sector services varies greatly by level of development (as is obvious from the examples discussed). For prosperous urban areas formal services are the norm; for low-income countries the formal services may be totally dwarfed by the informal sector, especially in rural areas, but even in some cities. What is critical is the realization that this hidden water and sanitation economy is extremely important in terms of both coverage and service. The informal sector offers many opportunities for providing services in an accountable, flexible way. When this is not possible because of economies of scale, service by the informal sector offers a major source of supplementary financing that can be redirected if the formal services can become more responsive to consumers' demands and perform in an efficient and accountable way.

The existence of the hidden water and sanitation economy has important implications for service provision. First, there is a high demand for services that has not been met successfully by the formal sector. Second, although some services are provided efficiently by the informal sector (as by tubewells in Pakistan), in other cases, such as water vending in the urban periphery, the costs of service are exorbitant. This is in large part attributable to the inability of informal providers to take advantage of the large economies of scale involved in transmitting water by pipe rather than by person or vehicle.

The specific implication for the formal sector is profound and clear: there is an enormous reservoir of resources that can be drawn on at reduced costs for all. This can happen when the formal sector is able to meet consumer demand and provide its services in a responsive, accountable way.

THE SCALE OF PUBLIC EXPENDITURE ON THE OLD AGENDA. The performance and sustainability of water and sanitation services depend not only on the level of financing for these services but also on the sources of such financing. Experience shows unequivocally that services are efficient and accountable to the degree that users are closely involved in providing financing for them. Or, stated another way, deficiencies in financing arrangements are a major source of the poor sector performance described earlier.

Figure 7. Sources of Financing in World Bank–Assisted Water and Sanitation Projects

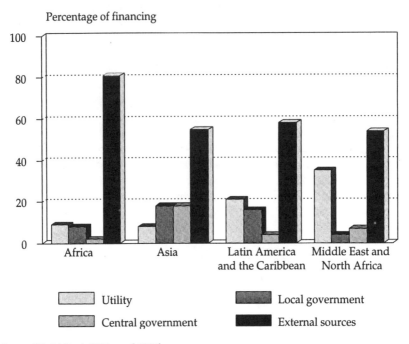

Source: World Bank 1991a and 1991b.

A World Bank analysis has assessed in detail the sources of financing for water and sanitation projects assisted by the World Bank. Internal cash generation in efficient, financially sustainable utilities is high—67 percent in a World Bank–assisted water and sewerage project in Valparaiso, Chile, for example. As shown in figure 7, there are wide regional differences in the relationship between financing and users. Africa has the longest way to go, with utilities and local government providing only 17 percent of investment financing. In the other three regions the proportion of financing mobilized by utilities themselves or received from local government is higher. In Asia the supply institutions generate relatively little financing, with central and local governments accounting for approximately equal shares. In the Middle East and North Africa utilities generate most of the domestic financing in World Bank–assisted projects, whereas in Latin America the contributions of the utilities and local government are similar. Unsatisfactory as these figures are, it appears that things are getting worse: internal cash generation financed 34 percent of the costs in World Bank–financed projects in 1988, 22 percent in 1989, 18 percent in 1990, and just 10 percent in 1991.

What Are the Keys to Developing a Financially Sustainable Sector?

An important backdrop to this discussion is the radical rethinking that has taken place and is still evolving in all aspects of economic development policy and natural resource policy. It is instructive to characterize an "old view" of sector policy (and the related financing challenges) deriving from the central planning model that dominated development thinking between the 1950s and the 1980s and contrast it with a "new view" that is emerging as a result of the emphasis on market-friendly policies and environmental sustainability.

The old view assumes that government has the primary responsibility for financing, managing, and operating services. It is government's task to define the services to be provided, to subsidize these services (especially for the poor), and to develop public organizations for service delivery. External support agencies are to assist this effort by providing the resource transfers necessary for service provision.

A remarkable consensus has been emerging in recent years for managing water resources and for delivering water supply and sanitation services on an efficient, equitable, and sustainable basis. At the heart of this consensus are two closely related guiding principles enunciated at the 1992 Dublin International Conference on Water and the Environment, which preceded the United Nations Conference on Environment and Development (UNCED—the "Earth Summit") the same year:

- Water has an economic value in all its competing uses and should be recognized as an economic good.
- Water development and management should be based on a participatory approach involving users, planners, and policymakers at all levels, with decisions taken at the lowest appropriate level.

These principles are now being widely adopted—for instance, in the World Bank's policy paper on water resources management and by the Development Assistance Committee of the Organization for Economic Cooperation and Development (OECD). The great challenges now facing the sector are articulation of the details implicit in these general principles and the translation of the Dublin principles into practice.

The new consensus gives prime importance to one central tenet (long familiar to students of public finance) that should underlie the financing of water resources management and water supply and sanitation services. According to this tenet, both efficiency and equity require that private financing be used for financing private goods and that public resources be used only for financing public goods. Implicit in the tenet is a belief that social units themselves—ranging, in this case, from households to river basin agencies—are in the best position to weigh the costs and benefits of different amounts of investment of resources for a particular level of social organization.

Figure 8. Levels of Decisionmaking on Water and Sanitation

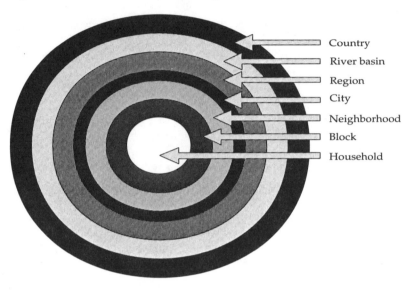

Country
River basin
Region
City
Neighborhood
Block
Household

The vital issue in application of this tenet to the water sector is the definition of the decision unit and of what is internal (private) and external (public) to that unit. Here it is useful to think of the different levels of units, as shown in figure 8. To illustrate the implications of the "decisionmaking rosette" (figure 8), it is instructive to consider how water supply and sanitation services should be financed.

FINANCING WATER SUPPLY SERVICES. The economic costs of providing water include (a) the financial costs of abstracting, transporting, storing, treating, and distributing the water and (b) the economic cost of water as an input. The latter cost arises because when water is taken, for example, from a stream for use in a city, other potential users are denied the possibility of using the water. The value of the most valuable opportunity foregone (known technically as the "scarcity value" or "opportunity cost") constitutes a legitimate element of the total production cost of water. In the most appropriate forms of water resources management (discussed later), charges based on the opportunity cost are levied on users. (As an empirical matter, the financial costs of water supplies to urban consumers and industries usually greatly exceed the opportunity costs. For low-value, high-volume uses—specifically, in irrigated agriculture—the relationship is frequently just the opposite;

opportunity costs are a considerable fraction of total costs, especially in situations of water scarcity.)

What of the benefit side? The provision of water supply to households carries several benefits. Households themselves value a convenient, reliable, and abundant water supply because of the time savings, amenity benefits, and, to a varying degree, health benefits. Because these "private" benefits constitute the bulk of the overall benefits of a household water supply, the public finance allocation principle dictates that most of the costs of such supplies should be borne by householders themselves. When this is the case, households make appropriate decisions on the type of service they want (for example, a communal tap, a yard tap, or multiple taps in the household). The corollary is that because this is principally a "private good," most of the financing for the provision of water supply services should be generated from user charges sufficient to cover the economic costs of inputs (including both the direct financial cost of inputs such as capital and labor and the opportunity cost of water as an input).

FINANCING SANITATION, SEWERAGE, AND WASTEWATER MANAGEMENT. The benefits from improved sanitation, and therefore the appropriate financing arrangements, are more complex. Households, the most basic level in figure 8, place high value on sanitation services that provide them with a private, convenient, odor-free facility which removes excreta and wastewater from the property or confines it appropriately within the property. However, there are clearly benefits that accrue at a more aggregate level and are therefore "externalities" from the point of view of the household. At the next level, the block, households in a particular block collectively place high value on services that remove excreta from the block as a whole. At the next level, the neighborhood, services that remove excreta and wastewater from the neighborhood or that render these wastes innocuous through treatment are valued. Similarly, at the city level the treatment of wastes or their removal from the environs of the city is valued.

Cities, however, do not exist in a vacuum; the wastes discharged from one city may pollute the water supply of a neighboring city. Accordingly, groups of cities (and farms and industries and others) in a river basin perceive a collective benefit from environmental improvement. Finally, because the health and well-being of a nation as a whole may be affected by environmental degradation in a particular river basin, there are sometimes additional national benefits from wastewater management in a particular basin.

The fundamental axiom of public financing prescribes that costs be assigned to different levels in this hierarchy according to the benefits accruing at different levels. This would suggest that the financing of sanitation, sewerage, and wastewater treatment be approximately as follows:

- Households pay the bulk of the costs incurred in providing on-plot facilities (bathrooms, toilets, on-lot sewerage connections).
- The residents of a block collectively pay the additional cost incurred in collecting the wastes from individual houses and transporting them to the boundary of the block.
- The residents of a neighborhood collectively pay the additional cost of collecting the wastes from blocks and transporting them to the boundary of the neighborhood (or of treating neighborhood wastes).
- The residents of a city collectively pay the additional cost of collecting the wastes from blocks and transporting them to the boundary of the city (or of treating the city wastes).
- The stakeholders in a river basin—cities, farmers, industries, and environmentalists—collectively assess the value of different levels of water quality within a basin, decide on the quality they wish to pay for, and determine the distribution of responsibility for paying for the necessary treatment and water quality management activities.

In practice, of course, there are complicating factors to be taken into account (including transaction costs of collection of revenues at different levels and the interconnectedness of several of the benefits). What is striking, nevertheless, is that the most innovative and successful forms of sector financing (and service provision) follow the above logic to a remarkable degree.

Box 1 described the financing of sewerage services in an informal urban settlement in Karachi. In this case households pay the costs of their on-lot services; blocks pay the cost of tertiary sewers; blocks pool their resources to pay for neighborhood (secondary) sewers; and the city (via the municipal development authority) pays for the trunk sewers. This evocative distinction between feeders and trunks is now being applied on a much larger scale to the provision of urban services in Pakistan.

The arrangements for the financing of condominial sewers by the urban poor in Brazil (box 3) follow similar lines: households pay on-lot costs, blocks pay for the block sewers (and decide what level of service they want), and the water company or municipality pays for the trunk sewers.

Even when the appropriate financing and institutional principles are followed, difficult issues arise with respect to financing wastewater treatment facilities. In industrial countries it is possible to discern two models that have been used.

Box 3. The Condominial Sewerage System in Brazil

The condominial system is the brain child of José Carlos de Melo, a socially committed engineer from Recife. The name "condominial" is applicable for two reasons: (a) the system treats a block of houses like a horizontal apartment building—condominial in Portuguese; and (b) "Condominial" was a popular Brazilian soap opera, associated with the best in urban life. As is evident in the box figure, the result is a layout radically different from the conventional system, with a shorter grid of smaller, shallower "feeder" sewers running through neighborhood backyards and with the effects of shallower connections to the mains rippling through the system. These innovations cut construction costs to between 20 and 30 percent those of a conventional system.

The more fundamental and radical innovation, however, is the active involvement of the population in choosing the level of service and in operating and maintaining the feeder infrastructure. The key elements are that families can choose: (a) to continue with their current sanitation system, (b) to connect to a conventional water-borne system, or (c) to connect to a condominial system. If a family chooses to connect to a condominial system, it has to pay a connection charge (financed by the water company) of, say, X cruzados and a monthly tariff of Y cruzados. If

Box figure. Schematic Layouts of Condominial and Conventional Sewerage Systems

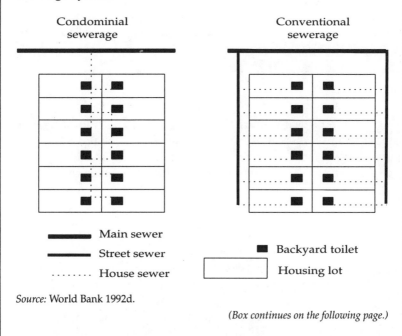

Condominial sewerage

Conventional sewerage

━━━ Main sewer
──── Street sewer
······· House sewer

■ Backyard toilet
☐ Housing lot

Source: World Bank 1992d.

(Box continues on the following page.)

Box 3 *(continued)*

it wants a conventional connection, it has to pay an initial cost of about 3X and a monthly tariff of 3Y (reflecting the different capital and operating costs). Families are free to continue with their current system, which usually means a holding tank discharging into an open street drain. In most cases, however, those families that initially choose not to connect eventually end up connecting. Either they succumb to heavy pressure from their neighbors or they find the buildup of wastewater in and around their houses intolerable once the (connected) neighbors fill in their stretches of the open drain.

Individual households are responsible for maintaining the feeder sewers, and the formal agency tends to the trunk mains only. This increases the communities' sense of responsibility for the system. Also, the misuse of any portion of the feeder system (by, say, putting solid waste down the toilet) soon shows up as a blockage in the neighbor's portion of the sewer. This leads to rapid, direct, and informed feedback to the misuser. The result is virtual elimination of the need to educate users in the do's and don'ts of the system and fewer blockages than in conventional systems. Finally, because of the utility's greatly reduced responsibility, its operating costs are sharply reduced.

The condominial system is now providing service to hundreds of thousands of urban people in northeast Brazil and is being replicated on a large scale throughout the country. Danger arises when the clever engineering is seen as the essence of "the system." Where the community and organizational aspects have been missing, the technology has worked poorly (as in Joinville, Santa Catarina) or not at all (as in the Baixada Fluminense in Rio de Janeiro).

In many industrial countries the approach has been to set universal standards and then to raise the funds necessary for financing the required investments. As is becoming increasingly evident, such an approach is turning out to be financially infeasible, even in the richest countries. In the United Kingdom the target date for compliance with the water quality standards of the European Union is being reviewed as customers' bills rise astronomically to pay the huge costs (over $60 billion projected for this decade) involved. In the United States local governments are revolting against the unfunded mandates of the federal government. A particularly pertinent case is the refusal of cities on the Pacific coast to spend the resources ($3 billion in the case of San Diego alone) required for secondary treatment of sewage. The U.S. National Academy of Sciences has advocated rescinding the "secondary treatment everywhere" mandate and developing an approach in which both costs and benefits are taken into account in the management of sewage in coastal areas.

In a few countries a different model has been developed. Institutional arrangements have been put into place that do three things: they ensure broad participation in the setting of standards and in making the tradeoffs between cost and water quality; they ensure that available resources are spent on those investments which yield the highest environmental return; and they use economic instruments to encourage both users and polluters to reduce the adverse environmental impact of their activities.

These principles, first applied immediately before World War I to the management of the Ruhr River Basin in Germany's industrial heartland, have provided the underpinnings for the management of the Ruhrverband ever since. Learning from its neighbor's experience, France developed a national river basin management system based on the Ruhrverband principles and has applied it since the early 1960s. Box 4 describes the principles of these river basin financing and management models. It shows how resources for wastewater treatment and water quality management are raised from users and polluters in a basin and how stakeholders—including users and polluters as well as citizens' groups—are involved in deciding the amount of resources to be raised and the level of environmental quality to be "purchased."[1] This system, which obviously embodies the central principles codified in the 1992 Dublin Statement, has proved extraordinarily efficient, robust, and flexible in meeting the financing needs of the densely industrialized Ruhr Valley for eighty-eight years and of France as a whole since the early 1960s.

There is growing evidence that if such workable, participatory agencies were developed, people in developing countries would be willing to pay substantial amounts for environmental improvement. In the Brazilian state of Espirito Santo a household survey showed that families were willing to pay 1.4 times the cost of sewage collection systems but 2.3 times the (higher) cost of a sewage collection and treatment system. In the Rio Doce Valley, an industrialized basin of nearly 3 million people in southeast Brazil, a French-type river basin authority is being developed. Stakeholders have indicated that they are willing to pay about $1 billion over a five-year period for environmental improvement. And in the Philippines recent surveys show that households are often prepared to make substantial payments for investments that will improve the quality of lakes and rivers.

For developing countries the implications of the experience of industrial countries are crystal clear. Even rich countries manage to treat only a part of their sewage; only 52 percent of sewage is treated in France and only 66 percent in Canada. Given the very low starting

Box 4. Water Resource Financing through River Basin Agencies in Germany and France

The Ruhrverband

The Ruhr area, with a population of about 5 million, contains the densest agglomeration of industrial and housing developments in Germany. The Ruhrverband, a self-governing public body, has managed water in the Ruhr Basin for eighty years. Its "associates" number 985 users (and polluters) of water, including communities, districts, and trade and industrial enterprises. The highest decisionmaking body of the Ruhrverband is the assembly of associates, which has the fundamental task of setting the budget (about $400 million annually), fixing standards, and deciding on the charges to be levied on users and polluters. The Ruhrverband itself is responsible for the "trunk infrastructure" (the design, construction, and operation of reservoirs and waste treatment facilities), while the communities are responsible for the "feeder infrastructure" (the collection of wastewater).

The French River Basin Financing Agencies

In the 1950s it became evident that France needed a new water resource management structure capable of successfully managing the emerging problems of water quality and quantity. The French modeled their system closely on the principles of the Ruhrverband but applied these principles nationwide. Each of the country's six river basins is governed by a basin committee (also known as a "water parliament") of between 60 and 110 persons who represent all stakeholders—national, regional, and local government industrial and agricultural interests, and citizens. The basin committee is supported by a technical and financial basin agency.

The technical tasks of the basin agency are to determine (a) how any particular level of financial resources should be spent (where treatment plants should be located, what level of treatment should be undertaken, and the like) so that environmental benefits are maximized, and (b) what level of environmental quality any particular level of financial resources can "buy." On the basis of this information, the basin committee determines the desired combination of costs and environmental quality for their (basin) society and how the services will be financed, relying heavily on charges levied on both users and polluters. The fundamental financial task of the basin agency is to administer the collection and distribution of the revenues.

In the French system (in contrast to the Ruhrverband) most of the resources collected are passed back to the municipalities and industries, which then invest in the agreed-on water and wastewater management facilities.

points in developing countries—only 2 percent of wastewater is treated in Latin America, for example—and the vital importance of improving the quality of the aquatic environment, what is needed is a process that will simultaneously make the best use of available resources and provide incentives to polluters to reduce the loads they impose on surface waters and groundwater.

Against this backdrop, developing countries face an awesome challenge. The old agenda—the provision of water supply and household sanitation services—is clearly a relatively "easy" task if sensible financial policies are adopted, since consumers want and are willing to pay for these services. Yet only a handful of developing countries have been successful in carrying out this "easy task" in an efficient, responsive, and financially sustainable way. The new agenda, which centers on management of wastewater and the environment, is a much more difficult and expensive undertaking, and one in which successes (in terms of efficiency and financial sustainability) are few and far between even in industrial countries.

There is heartening evidence that the right lessons are being drawn from the experiences of many industrial countries. Just five years ago the Baltic Sea Clean-Up was conceived of in classic terms—setting quality standards and then determining what was needed to finance the needed investments. When the calculations were done, it became clear that the necessary money (over $20 billion) could not possibly be raised. At the Interministerial Conference on Financing of the Baltic Sea Clean-Up, held in Gdansk in 1993, this approach was abandoned for a far more productive one: ensuring that the limited available resources were invested in such a way as to develop financially sustainable and efficient water and sanitation utilities and that the limited resources for wastewater treatment were allocated to the highest-priority investments.

Daunting as the new agenda is, there is cause for hope. It is encouraging that delegates from more than 100 countries could agree at the Dublin conference on the global relevance of the principles underlying the Ruhr and French water resource management systems. Even more important are the signs that the Ruhr/French system is now being adopted, with appropriate modifications, in Brazil, Indonesia, Poland, Spain, and Venezuela and is likely to be applied in many developing countries in the near future.

SOME COMMON MISCONCEPTIONS ABOUT THE NEW APPROACH TO FINANCING. Finally, it is important to explore three common misconceptions that may impede the adoption of the "new" financing perspective:

- *Misconception 1. The existence of externalities means that a demand-based, participatory approach to sector development cannot work.*

It is frequently asserted that a demand-based approach is fine for "private goods" but not for "public goods" such as environmental quality. An important point on this score is that a central feature of the approach advocated here is respect for the capacity of stakeholders to make the right decisions. The principle which applies at the household level—that the household is in the best position to decide how to spend the resources available to it—can be successively applied at higher levels of social aggregation to solve the resource allocation issues appropriate to those levels.[2] And the basic behavioral-based decision process is not to be overridden by appealing to "externalities." At any particular level, externalities are dealt with by "kicking them up" one step, where they are internalized.[3] Finally, a successively smaller and smaller number of decisions need to be made at higher levels.

There is clear evidence from the experience of the World Bank that the (appropriate) concern with environmental quality can easily lead to a supply-driven approach which mandates investments on the basis of technocratic criteria. Such an approach ends up serving the interests of consultants and contractors rather than of the people who use the services or of the environment in which they live. In such a context, it has correctly been asserted that "externalities are the first refuge of scoundrels!"

- *Misconception 2. The new approach to financing does not address the needs of the poor.*

A second myth about the new approach to financing is that it does not take adequate account of the situation of the poor and their need for subsidies. The justification usually offered for high levels of public financing for water and sanitation services in developing countries is the low ability of poor people to pay for services. In practice, however, it is the rich, not the poor, who virtually always benefit disproportionately from subsidized water and sanitation services.

As described earlier, unserved people, particularly those in urban areas, pay much higher prices for water. And it is the poor who are the unserved. Figure 9 reports the results of a detailed assessment of who benefits from public subsidies of water supply and sanitation services in several Latin American countries. The results are striking and the conclusions clear—although subsidies are justified as "being necessary because poor people cannot afford to pay," they end up heavily favoring the rich, with the inequity directly related to the degree of rationing of the service. Inequity is, accordingly, greater in low- than in middle-income countries, and greater for sewerage than for water supply.

The cycle is clear. Where services are heavily subsidized, service expansion is relatively slow, both because the available resources are used inefficiently—which can be traced to the supply organizations

Figure 9. Who Benefits from Subsidized Water and Sanitation Services in Latin America

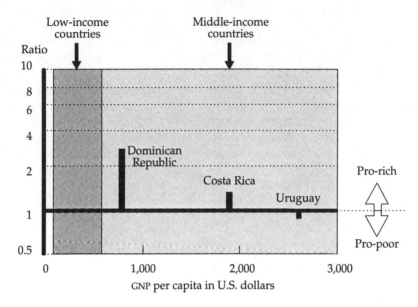

Water supply

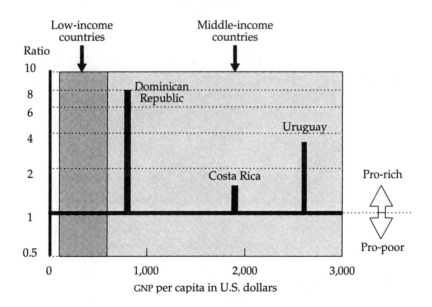

Sewerage

Source: Petrie 1989.

not being directly accountable to their customers—and because of constraints on public financing. The consequence is that "the lucky ones" get subsidized services while "the unlucky ones" who are not served pay an exorbitant human, social, and financial price to get services. Data from Latin America (see figure 9) provide confirmation of the universal rule that "luck" is not a random outcome but is the prerogative of the privileged. These data also show that inequities are greatest where services are most heavily rationed: in the poorest countries, and for sewerage. (This has appropriately been termed "the hydraulic law of subsidies"—the subsidies go with the service, and it will always be the better off and more influential who, public pronouncements notwithstanding, benefit first. And it will always be the less influential— the poor—who are at the end of the line both literally and figuratively and who either do not get services or suffer most from poor-quality services.)

If subsidized services do not make sense, does it follow that we should abandon the poor? The answer is an unequivocal no. Although

Figure 10. How Spreading Connection Costs over Time Affects Connection Rates in Kerala, India

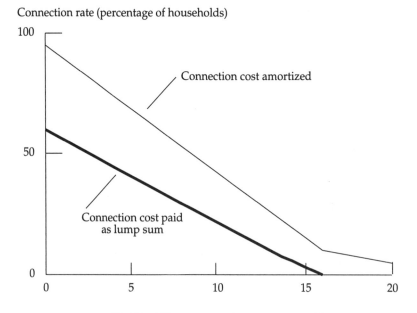

Connection rate (percentage of households)

Tariff paid by customer (rupees per month)

Source: World Bank 1992d.

subsidies often (as in the above case) work perversely in practice, t. transfer of resources to poor people is obviously a legitimate and desirable instrument of public policy. The key is to resist the temptation to earmark those transfers for particular types of services (which the poor may or may not value). Once again this comes down to the question of trusting people—even poor people—to know how best to spend the resources available to them. In practice, then, where block grants are made to poor communities, the communities themselves can choose whether to use the funds for water and sewerage services. This practice is becoming fairly widespread with the social development funds that have become common in developing countries in recent years.

The poor often face considerable difficulties in raising the capital required for the initial costs of connecting to a piped water supply system. Studies in India and Pakistan (figure 10) have shown that connection rates can be increased substantially if water companies provide financing (not subsidies) to poor customers for the costs of connecting to piped systems. The experience of the Grameen Bank in Bangladesh (box 5) shows that more people—and especially poor people—will make use of improved supplies if supply agencies can help consumers in spreading initial costs over time. This practice of amortizing the costs of connections over, typically, five years has met with considerable success in Latin America for many years.

Box 5. How the Grameen Bank Finances Rural Water Supply in Bangladesh

The Grameen Bank is well known as a provider of credit to more than 2 million poor and landless people in Bangladesh. A large proportion of the clients of the bank are women. The bank's great innovation has been to find an alternative to traditional forms of collateral. The key principle is that if any borrower defaults, the group to which that borrower belongs is no longer considered creditworthy and is no longer eligible for loans.

In recent years the lending of the Grameen Bank for rural water supplies has risen dramatically. Since early 1992 the bank has provided loans for about 70,000 tubewells. In 1993 it lent about $16 million. The interest rate charged on loans for tubewells is 20 percent, repayable over two years in weekly installments. The handpumps are procured locally by the borrowers, either from the Public Health Engineering Department or from local private manufacturers.

Source: United Nations Children's Fund (UNICEF) data.

Misconception 3. The financing problem can be overcome by mobilizing financing from the private sector.

Faced with constraints on public financing, some countries have looked to the private sector to finance the massive investments required. There are many reasons—efficiency, innovation, and separation of provider and regulator—suggesting that it is often appropriate to involve the private sector in the provision of these services. And instances of private sector financing being mobilized for wastewater investments (especially for build-operate-transfer schemes) are multiplying, in Indonesia, Malaysia, Mexico, and other developing countries.

A major factor has to to be taken into account in assessing the role of the private sector in financing wastewater investments in developing countries. As shown in figure 11, public facility projects are often:

> characterized by a long construction period, followed by a gradual increase in the revenue extracted from the operation, with the result that the investors may have to wait 8 to 10 years before receiving their first dividend and will almost have to wait 15 to 20 years before obtaining a rate of return comparable to that offered by an in-

Figure 11. Time Profile of Expenses and Receipts for Typical Infrastructure Investments

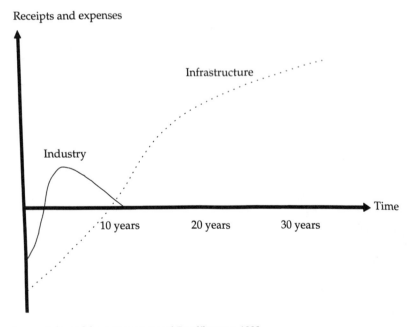

Source: Adapted from Davezies and Prud'homme 1993.

Table 3. Private and Public Financing of Privately Operated Water and Sewerage Services in France (Approximate)

(percent)

	Water supply	Sewerage
Public financing	30	70
Private financing	70	30
All delegated management	100	100

Source: Lyonnais des Eaux, Paris, data 1992.

dustrial investment. In addition, the entire construction period may be characterized by considerable uncertainty about the ultimate profitability of the investment (because of potential cost overruns and because of the uncertainty about operating revenues). During this period of great uncertainty, remuneration of the investor's risk should compare to that of venture capital and run at the level of 25 to 30 percent. In contrast, when tariff levels are known following commencement of operation, revenues are not likely to vary as much as in an industrial project. The risk (and appropriate return) is thus less (Davezies and Prud'homme 1993).

Three observations are relevant in this context. First (see table 3), in France, the country with the longest history of private sector participation in the water sector, the bulk of privately operated water supplies is privately financed (concession contracts), but most privately operated sewerage is publicly financed (affermage contracts). Second, where capital markets are relatively shallow—as is the case in most developing countries—the transition from public financing to long-term private financing is going to take time and ingenuity. And third, because the investment costs are so large, cost recovery frequently has to be scheduled over a number of years.

Conclusion

We can now sum up the financing challenges that face us in this sector. First, we need to complete the old agenda. It is clear that the bulk of financing can and should come from users. For this to happen, attention has to be given to both demand-side and supply-side factors. On the demand side there must be a rigorous focus on providing the services that people want and are willing to pay for. Above all, this means changing from the "we know best" attitude that has characterized the sector for too long to a focus on meeting households' needs as the households themselves see them. On the supply side the focus must be on developing institutional arrangements that provide services at least cost and in a way that is responsive and accountable to consumers. The examples we have discussed provide some indications of the most promising directions. In many cases this will involve partnerships in which "nonformal institutions" (such as neighborhood associations) manage the feeder infrastructure and "formal institutions" (such as utilities) manage the trunk infrastructure. In many other cases it will involve a much greater role for the private sector in the provision of services, via both nonformal and formal institutions.

Second, we need to embark on the new agenda. Here the challenge for developing countries is enormous. As this booklet has stressed, financial realities are forcing industrial countries to make difficult choices about how much investment to make in preserving the aquatic environment and how to spend the available resources. In developing countries the situation is much more difficult for three reasons: the challenge has to be met while the old agenda is still on the table; aquatic environmental quality is much worse in developing countries; and developing countries have far fewer resources to devote to environmental protection. What this means is that developing countries and those who support them have to confront very difficult tradeoffs and make many tough decisions.

Finally, we need to step back from the dry intricacies of financing and put the discussion in a broader context. The overriding challenge to the developing world today is to improve the well-being of the poor in a way that is both environmentally and financially sustainable. Awesome as this challenge is, we can now discern an emerging consensus on what needs to be done and how to do it.

The consensus involves three key ideas. The first, the most mundane, is that the reduction of poverty depends in a fundamental way on sound economic policies, which means fiscal common sense and the maximum use of the market and market-like instruments. The second idea is one that has come to the fore recently. It is that the only true development is one in which economic progress and environmental enhancement go hand in hand and are mutually reinforcing. The third idea is both fundamental and radical. It is that people have to be not only the object but the subject of development. It is the people themselves—all the people—who have to decide what services they want; it is the people to whom service institutions have to be responsive and accountable; it is the affected people who have to make the decisions (based on information from technicians) on environmental policies and standards.

The consensus around these simple and powerful ideas opens up exciting prospects for making large and sustainable progress in improving the lives of people in developing countries. In this booklet, we have traced the implications of these ideas for the water and sanitation sector.

We are greatly encouraged by the emerging consensus exemplified in the Dublin Statement and the freshwater chapter of *Agenda 21*. We recognize that there is much to be done and much to be learned. This will require concerted effort from us all. The World Bank is committed to working with its partners in the development community and with the people of the developing world in translating this consensus into actions to improve the lives of billions of people who lack adequate water and sanitation services and billions who live in degraded environments throughout the developing world.

Notes

1. With respect to the discussion of freshwater in *Agenda 21*, the key document of UNCED, the administrative and technical budgets of the river basin agencies in France and Germany are also decided on by the governing "water parliaments." See section A, Integrated Water Resources Management and Development, and section B, Protection of Water Resources, Water Quality and Aquatic Ecosystems, in the chapter on "Freshwater" in *Agenda 21*.

2. The critical concept here is that one party's externalities are another party's costs (or benefits).

3. The situation is similar for health benefits, as discussed in World Bank (1993b), pp. 92–95.

References

Brazil, Direccao Nacional de Aguas e Energia. 1992. Projeto Rio Doce. Brasilia.

DANIDA (Danish International Development Agency). 1991. *The Copenhagen Report, Implementation Mechanisms for Integrated Water Resources Development and Management.* Copenhagen: Ministry of Foreign Affairs, Copenhagen.

Davezies, L. and Remy Prud'homme. 1993. "The Economics of Public-Private Partnership in Infrastructure." In Claude Martinand, ed., *Private Financing of Public Infrastructure: The French Experience. Paris: Ministry of Public Works, Transportation and Tourism.*

de Melo, Jose Carlos. 1985. "Sistemas Condominiais de Esgotos," *Engenharia Sanitaria* 24(2): 237–38.

Garn, Harvey A. 1987. "Patterns in the Data Reported on Completed Water Supply Projects." World Bank, Infrastructure and Urban Development Department, Water Supply and Sanitation Division, Washington D.C.

———. 1990. "Financing Water Supply and Sanitation Services." Prepared for the Collaborative Council as a background paper for the Delhi Conference. World Bank, Infrastructure and Urban Development Department, Water Supply and Sanitation Division, World Bank, Washington, DC.

Hasan, Arif. 1986. "Innovative Sewerage in a Karachi Squatter Settlement: The Low-Cost Sanitation Programme of the Orangi Pilot Project and the Process of Change in Orangi." Orangi Pilot Project, Karachi

———. 1990. "Community Groups and NGOs in the Urban Field in Pakistan." *Environment and Urbanization.* 2: 74–86.

India, Planning Commission. 1992. "Water Supply and Sanitation." In *The Eighth Five Year Plan (1992–97).* New Delhi.

India, Ministry of Urban Development. 1993. Proceedings of National Conference of Urban Water Supply and Sanitation Policy. New Delhi.

International Conference on Water and the Environment. 1992. "The Dublin Statement and Report of the Conference." Dublin.

Petrei, A. H. 1989. *El Gasto Publico Social y sus Efectos Distributivos.* Santiago: ECIEL.

Ruhrverband. 1992. "Tasks and Structure." Essen.

Singh, Bhanwar, Radhika Ramasubban, Ramesh Bhatia, John Briscoe, Charles C. Griffin, and Chongchun Kim. 1993. "Rural Water Supply in Kerala, India: How to Emerge From a Low-Level Equilibrium Trap." *Water Resources Research* 29(7): 1931–42.

United Nations Commission on Sustainable Development. 1994. "Financing of Freshwater for Sustainable Development." Background Paper 5 for the Intersessional Ad Hoc Working Group on Finance. New York.

U.S. National Research Council. 1994. *Wastewater Management for Coastal Urban Areas.* Water Science and Technology Board. Washington, D.C.

"Warning on costs of European Union 'Green' Law," *Financial Times*, 21 February 1994, p. 8.

Watson, Gabrielle. 1992. "Water and Sanitation in Sâo Paulo, Brazil; Successful Strategies for Service Provision in Low-Income Communities." Master's thesis in city planning, Massachusetts Institute of Technology, Cambridge. Mass.

World Bank. 1988. "FY88 Annual Sector Review—Water Supply and Sanitation." World Bank, Infrastructure and Urban Development Department, Water and Sanitation Division, Washington, D.C.

———. 1991a. "FY90 Sector Review—Water Supply and Sanitation." World Bank, Infrastructure and Urban Development Department, Water and Sanitation Division, Washington, D.C.

———. 1991b. "FY91 Sector Review—Water Supply and Sanitation." World Bank, Infrastructure and Urban Development Department, Water and Sanitation Division, Washington, D.C.

———. 1992a. "FY92 Sector Review—Water Supply and Sanitation," World Bank, Infrastructure and Urban Development Department, Water and Sanitation Division, Washington, D.C.

———. 1992b. "Utility Reform and Environmental Clean-up in Formerly Socialist Countries: Report of a Workshop on the Baltic Sea." Water and Sanitation Utilities Partnership Report 3, World Bank, Infrastructure and Urban Development Department, Water and Sanitation Division, Washington D.C.

———. 1992c. *Water Supply and Sanitation Projects: The Bank's Experience, 1967–1989*, World Bank, Operations Evaluation Department, Washington, D.C.

———. 1992d. *World Development Report 1992: Development and the Environment.* New York: Oxford University Press.

———. 1993a. *Water Resources Management.* A World Bank Policy Paper. Washington, D.C.

———. 1993b. *World Development Report 1993: Investing in Health.* New York: Oxford University Press.

———. 1994. *World Development Report 1994: Investing in Infrastructure.* New York: Oxford University Press.

World Bank Water Demand Research Team. 1993. "The Demand for Water in Rural Areas: Determinants and Policy Implications." World Bank Research Observer 8 (1): 47–70.

Yepes, Guillermo. 1991. "Water Supply and Sanitation Sector Maintenance: The Costs of Neglect and Options to Improve It." World Bank, Latin America and Caribbean Region Technical Department, Washington, D.C.